Learn To Code

The Beginner's Guide to Computer Programming

Dave Jones

Book Description

As the title suggests, "Learn To Code: The Beginner's Guide to Computer Programming" will help you learn how to code and possibly try to make a career out of it.

Programming can be difficult to learn, but once you get a good grasp of it, you will never stop. If you are wondering why many programmers stay at night and even work countless hours, it is because programming can be really exciting.

You can learn how to see programming that way through this book. This will help you to:

- Understand why programming is a highly-valued skill in today's world
- Know the fundamental theories behind programming
- Learn Python - the easiest programming language yet
- Identify the skills and the tools you need to help you learn how to code
- And most importantly how to find a job as a programmer with no experience and with no Computer Science degree

Table of Contents

PART I - THE BASICS

Chapter 1 - Why Learn How to Code?

Coding is a great example of how you can apply math and sciences, because it will teach you how to take an iterative method in testing out ideas and solving problems. Some have purchased this book as a stepping stone in their career as a professional coder, while other people have read this book to try to learn a new skill. Regardless, you will find that coding can significantly improve your problem-solving skills.

Now that a huge part of our lives is being run by software through automating all types of processes, the fundamental skill of how strings of text can build the electronic world that we live on is becoming a necessity to become digitally literate.

Coding is a highly-valued skill nowadays, as everyone cannot do it. Even if you are not eyeing to become a professional programmer, you can sharpen your ability to solve problems by learning how to code.

Most programs that we now use every day could be programmed in some way. For example, Excel can allow you to create basic macros to help you with spreadsheets. The MacOS can also be programmed to automate some of the features using AppleScript. Meanwhile, Adobe programs such as After Effects, Illustrator, and PhotoShop could be automated through JavaScript. There is a high chance that you are using an application that once you learn how to code, can help you perform your tasks faster and better.

There are regular office guys who have got promoted, because they have learned how to code. Some employees have managed to program all types of small applications that helped them with their work performance. For instance, one office clerk had to work with different types of financial data. He thought about getting a new perspective of this data, so he wrote a small code using JavaScript, which could read the data, show a new column of statistics with results that are color-coded. This helped the regular office clerk to be promoted as a senior data analyst.

Another example is a small business owner who had to fill out inventory forms manually each week. Because he learned how to code and he doesn't have the budget yet to purchase a sophisticated inventory system software, he created a program that helps him to manage inventory through PHP.

There are many forms of programs that you can write. Some may take several minutes to write, some may take weeks and even years. However, it will end up saving your hours of mindless tasks. But more than just solving everyday work problems, coding can be really fun. This is problem solving in action. And even though building a business though coding such as Twitter or Instagram will definitely require a lot of coding experience, these simple programs that we have cited here don't. As a matter of fact, it can be really exciting to create a simple program to solve your everyday woes.

Whether you want to be a professional programmer or you want to add coding as a skill to boost up your CV, you can achieve exciting things when you start learning how to code. In this book, we will learn the fundamental concepts of coding, and how you can make a career out of it, if you choose to be.

Chapter 2 - Prepare Yourself to Code

There are many ways how to code and there are many programming languages you can use. Hence, the first thing that you should consider is which language you should use. Are you interested in creating apps for handheld devices? Do you want to build websites? You can also learn how to code so you can know how you can program computers that are integrated with TV, car, or even your fridge. Try to determine the result you want as each area may require different set of code. While this book cannot cover every form and type of coding, you will learn where to begin looking.

If you want to learn code so you can become a professional, there a high chance that you need to work with the languages often used in schools such as Java and PHP. Meanwhile, if you want to learn how to code so you can use your programming skills in the actual work setting, this book will cover the basic areas for languages that are commonly used in different industries for different purposes.

Python

To help you learn how to code, and for the purpose of instruction, we will use Python in this book. Programming languages have their own principles, cultures, and ecosystems built around them. It will be an extra challenge for you if you choose a language that is different from the language commonly used in your workplace. For example, if you are trying to get a job in Facebook, Google, or Twitter, you have to learn Python as this is the programming language used in these places.

Basically, the cultural values of Python revolves around being an open source software, community involvement, and most importantly teaching new coders. If you think this is a good fit for your goal of learning how to code, Python can be a good fit.

A programmer with enough experience in any programming language can easily learn Python. It is also quite easy for non-programmers to learn and use. You can easily install Python, and most UNIX and Linux distributions are already packed with the latest version of Python. Even some Windows PC are already installed with Python.

You can download the latest version of Python software by clicking this link:

https://wiki.python.org/moin/BeginnersGuide/Download

Learning How to Code with Python

Before you start, you have to determine with text editors and IDEs are ideal to make it easy for you to edit Python codes. The Python website has a list of code samples as well as introductory manuals that you will find helpful.

Minimum Hardware Requirements for Coding

Basically, any decent computer can effectively run the Python software. But if you need more specific guidelines, you can try to obtain the following specifications for laptops and desktops.

For laptop computers, I recommend the following minimum requirements to successfully use Python:

Processor: Intel Core 13
Operating System: Microsoft Windows 7 Professional x64
Storage: 500 GB internal hard drive
Memory: 4 GB RAM

Monitor: 13" LCD Monitor
CD-ROM: DVD/CD-RW

For desktop computers, I recommend the following minimum requirements:

Processor: Intel Core 13
Operating System: Microsoft Windows 7 Professional x64
Storage: 500 GB internal hard drive
Memory: 4 GB RAM
Monitor: 135 LCD Monitor
CD-ROM: DVD/CD-RW
Dual-band WiFi-certified 802.11 a/g - compliant adapter

Chapter 3 - Introduction to Python Programming

Programming is defined as the process of writing a code using a specific type of language, in this book Python, so it can be performed by a computer. Even though there are several programming languages, and numerous forms of computers, you first need to define the solution. Without the solution, in form of an algorithm, a program cannot exist.

Algorithm refers to the solution to a problem in terms of the data required to signify the problem as well as the steps needed to come up with the expected result. As a programming language, Python presents a notational way to present both the data and the process.

Programming with Python

Python is regarded as the simplest programming language yet, mainly because it has a very straightforward syntax. It promotes programming without the need for prepared code.

The print directive is the simplest directive, which you can find in most Python tutorials. It simply directs the computer to print out a line and include a new line. Take note that there are two primary version of Python - Python 2 & Python 3, which are not similar. In this book, we are using Python 3, because it has newer features and I find it more semantically accurate than Python 2.

One good example is the print directive. In Python 2, this is not a function, and so you can use it without parentheses. But in Python 3, this is already a function, so you should use it with parentheses.

```
1   print("I am learning Python")
```

The result will be:

```
I am learning Python

In [1]:
```

Indentation

Instead of curly braces, you need to use indentation for blocks. You can use both the spacebar and the tabs for indentation. However, you may need to use four spaces for standard indentation:

```
1   x = 1
2 ▾ if x == 1:
3       # four space indentation
4       print("x is 1.")
```

```
x is 1.

In [1]:
```

Chapter 4 - Functions

In programming, functions are used to divide the code into functional groups or blocks, which will allow you to make the code more readable and more organized. The blocks of codes can also be used, which will save you a lot of time. In addition, functions are important if you want to define the interface in your program and share your code to other programmers.

Functions in Python

Like most programming languages, Python also uses functions. In using Python, the block is a specific area of code, which is written in the following format:

```
1 ▾ block_header:
2       First block line
3       Second block line
4       ...|
```

The block line refers to a Python code, while the block head should be written in the format as:

block_keyword block_name(argument1, argument2, ...)

The common block keywords used in Python are "for", "if", and "while".

The block keyword "def" defines the functions in Python. This is normally followed with the name of the function as the name of the block, as shown in the example below:

9

```
1 ▾ def my_function():
2       print("Hello Python!")
```

You can also enable the functions in Python to receive arguments, which are variables passed from the caller to the function as shown below:

```
1 ▾ def my_function_with_args(username, greeting):
2       print("Hello, %s , From Python!, I wish you %s"%(username
    , greeting))
```

You can also return a value to the caller using functions through the keyword 'return' as shown in the example below:

```
1 ▾ def sum_two_numbers(a, b):
2       return a + b
```

In order to call functions in Python, you need to write the name of the specific function within parentheses. You have to place the specific argument inside the brackets. As an example, we can call the functions above:

```
1    # Define our 3 functions
2 ▾  def my_function():
3        print("Hello Python!")
4
5 ▾  def my_function_with_args(username, greeting):
6        print("Hello, %s , From Python!, I wish you %s"%
     (username, greeting))
7
8 ▾  def sum_two_numbers(a, b):
9        return a + b
10
11   # print(a simple greeting)
12   my_function()
13
14   #prints - "Hello, John Smith, From Python!, I wish you a
     great year!"
15   my_function_with_args("John Smith", "Merry Christmas!")
16
17   # after this line x will hold the value 3!
18   x = sum_two_numbers(1,2)
```

Chapter 5 - Containers

Among the benefits of Python as a programming language is its simplicity to control containers. Also known as collections, containers are crucial part of coding and they are already integrated in the syntax of most coding languages. We can say that thinking in a Pythonic approach is perceiving the programming in terms of containers.

Lists

As a container, lists in programming manifest a mutable, ordered collection of objects. You could mix and match any form of object in a list, add more items, or discard any item on your will. An empty list can be created by using square brackets. Alternatively, you can also use the list() function without the arguments.

```
>>> l = []
>>> l
[]
>>> l = list()
>>> l
[]
```

Meanwhile, you could initialize list with any form of content through the square bracket notation. The function list() also takes an iterable as a single argument and will return a shallow copy of this new list.

```
>>> l = ['x', 'y', 'z']
    >>> l
    ['x', 'y', 'z']
    >>> l2 = list(l)
    >>> l2
    ['x', 'y', 'z']
```

It is easy to iterate over a list. Take note that in Python, all the iterables will allow you to access factors using the statement for...in. Following this format, every element in the iterable can be assigned sequentially to the variable loop for a single entry of the loop contained in the block.

```
>>> for letter in l:
...       print letter,
...
X y z
```

A character sequence can also be Python string and regarded as iterable containers enclosing the codes. You can easily create a new list of characters when you combine strings with the list() function.

```
>>> list('uvwxyz')

    ['u', 'v', 'w', 'x', 'y', 'z']
```

A newline character will be added if you call the print statement. You can use the trail "," in this statement to avoid automatic appending a newline character.

You can also iterate with the while loop for a specific iteration. Remember, a while loop is a commonly used loop to execute an iteration of any length, either by verifying a condition on every entry or by using a break statement to close the code once it meets the requirements.

13

Below is a simple example that uses the method lis.pop() to run through the list from right to left:

```
>>> l = ['x', 'y', 'z']
>>> while len(l):
...     print l.pop(),
...
z y x
```

Chapter 6 - String Manipulation

String refers to the type of object, which is composed of a character sequence. It is already integrated with Python to understand how it could deal with strings. In Python, you can manipulate the strings via string operators, which are represented by familiar mathematical symbols: +, - , * , = , and /.

When we say concatenate, it means you have to combine two or more strings, which you can do by using the operator +. Remember, you should be clear on where you like the space to occur by adding them between the quote marks.

The example below shows the content "hello Python" for the string "phrase 1"

```
phrase1 = 'hello' + ' ' + 'Python'
        print(phrase1)
        -> hello Python
```

The example below shows the content "hello Python" for the string "phrase 1"

If you like several copies of a specific string, you can use the operator *. In our example below, the string phrase2a is assigned the content "hello" two times. Meanwhile, phrase2b is assigned content "Python", then we order the code to print both strings.

```
phrase2a = 'hello ' * 2
phrase2b = 'Python'
print(phrase2a + phrase2b)
-> hello hello Python
```

You can use the operator += if you need to add an item to the end of a string:

```
phrase3 = 'Thanks'
phrase3 += ' '
phrase3 += 'Python'
print(message3)
-> Thanks Python
```

Aside from operators, Python is added with several string methods, which will allow you to manipulate strings. Either as a standalone command or as an added code, these string methods can modify the strings. You can refer to the Python website for the list of these string methods, which includes specific information on how you can use each method.

For example, a common string method is find, which allows you to lookup a string for a substring. Python will provide you with a starting index position of a specific substring. This will help you greatly if you move into advanced programming. Take note that the count begins with zero and not 1, and the indexes are numbered from left to right.

```
phrase5 = "hello Python"
phrase5a = phrase5.find("Pyth")
print(phrase5a)
-> 5
```

When the substirng is non-existent, Python will return -1 as a value.

```
phrase6 = "Hello World"
phrase6b = phrase6.find("java")
print(phrase6b)
-> -1
```

Chapter 7 - Loops

In programming, statements are performed in sequence - the first statement will be performed first, the second statement will be next, followed by the third statement, and so on. There might be instances when you have to perform a block of code several times. In any programming language, you can use different control structures, which allow for more sophisticated paths.

Below is an example of a loop in Python:

```
1    primes = [2, 3, 5, 7]
2 ▾  for prime in primes:
3        print(prime)
```

Basically, loop statements will allow the code to perform a statement or blocks several times. In Python, the following are the most common types of loops:

For Loop

Perform a series of statements several times and abbreviate the code, which will manage the loop variable.

A for loop statement could iterate over a series of numbers through the "range" and "xrange" functions. The key difference between the xrange and the range is that the latter can return a new list with numbers of that particular range, while the xrange returns an iterator that is more effective. Take note that Python 3 is using the range function that behaves like the xrange function, and that the range function has a zero base.

```
1    # Prints out the numbers 0,1,2,3,4
2 ▾  for x in range(5):
3        print(x)
4
5    # Prints out 3,4,5
6 ▾  for x in range(3, 6):
7        print(x)
8
9    # Prints out 3,5,7
10 ▾ for x in range(3, 8, 2):
11       print(x)
```

While Loop

This loop repeats a statement or block of statements while a specific condition is met. The program can confirm the condition before performing the loop block. To put it simply, a while loop statement repeats the sequence as long as a specific boolean condition is present. For example:

```
1    # Prints out 0,1,2,3,4
2
3    count = 0
4 ▾  while count < 5:
5        print(count)
6        count += 1   # This is the same as count = count + 1
```

Nested Loops

It is possible to use one or several loops within any for, while or do...while loop

On the other hand, loop control statements are used to change the execution of the code from its regular sequence. If the execution leaves a scope, the rest of the automated objects that were contained in that scope will be deleted.

In Python, you can use the following control statements:

Break Statement

This control statement cancels the loop statement and transmits execution to the statement right after the following loop.

Continue Statement

This statement will allow the loop to skip the rest of its block and easily reconfirm its condition before reiteration.

Pass Statement

This statement is used if a statement is needed syntactically, but you don't like any code or command to proceed with execution.

Chapter 8 - Modules

Modules will allow you to systematically organize your codes by categorizing related code into a module. This process makes the code easier to use and understand. Modules are Python objects with arbitrarily named attributes, which you can reference and bind. Basically, a module is a file composed of Python code and could be define variables, classes, and functions. A runnable code can also be integrated into a module.

When you first load a module into a current Python script, the program will initialize the codes in the module one time. If you want to import the urlib module, you can just import the module so you can create and read data from specified URLs.

```
1   # import the library
2   import urllib
3
4   # use it
5   urllib.urlopen(...)
```

An import statement allows you to use any Python source file. This can be done by executing an import statement in some other source file. Below is the syntax for import statement:

```
import module1[, module2[,... moduleN]
```

The interpreter imports the module if the module is present in the search path and when it encounters an import statement. A search path refers to the list of directories, which the interpreter could search prior to importing a module. For instance, in order to import the module support.py, you have to include the following code on the upper part of the script:

```
#!/usr/bin/python

# Import module support
import support

# Now you can call defined function that module as follows
support.print_func("Sabrina")
```

If you run the code above, the result will be:

```
Hello : Sabrina
```

Take note that a module can only be loaded once, regardless of the frequency of its import. This will prevent the execution of the module from happening several times if there are instances of several imports.

Chapter 9 - Files

Using the print statement is the simplest method to generate output. This statement can process zero or more expressions, which are divided using comma. The print function transforms the expressions you transfer to strings and will code the output to a standard output:

```
#!/usr/bin/python

print "Python is easy to learn,", "right?"
```

The output will appear as:

```
        Python is easy to learn, right?
```

In Python, you have two integrated functions that will read the text line coming from the basic input, which is by default can be added using your keyboard: input and raw_input.

The input function behaves like a raw_input, except that it has an assumption that the input is a valid expression for Python and returns the confirmed result to you.

```
#!/usr/bin/python

str = input("Add your input: ");
print "Final input is : ", str
```

This will result to the following input:

```
Add your input: [x*5 for x in range(2,10,2)]
Final input is :  [10, 20, 30, 40]
```

Meanwhile, the raw input Function interprets a single line generated by the standard input and process it as a string.

```
#!/usr/bin/python

str = raw_input("Add your input: ");
print "Final input is : ", str
```

This will prompt the program to add a string, and it will return the string on the terminal. If you add "Howdy Partner!", it will appear like this:

```
Add your input: Howdy Partner!
Final input is :  Howdy Partner!
```

At this point, we have been interpreting the standard output and input. It is time to see how we can use actual files in Python. In this language, you can use fundamental methods and functions needed to manipulate the files.

However, prior to writing or reading a data file, you need to open it by using the open() function, which is a built-in function in Python. This function will allow you to create a file object that will be used in calling other related support methods.

Below is the syntax for opening files in Python:

```
file object = open(file_name [, access_mode][, buffering])
```

The file_name is an argument and a value string, which keeps the file name that you want to access.

On the other hand, the access_mode defines the mode wherein the data file should be opened such as append, write, or read. You can visit the Python website to access the complete array of potential values.

Take note that (r) or read is the default access file.

Chapter 10 - Bringing It All Together

At this point, we have already covered the fundamental concepts of programming using the Python language. In summary, the first part of the book helped us to learn the following:

- Learning how to code is your first step towards a rewarding and exciting career. Even if you decide not to be a professional programmer, your problem solving skills can be greatly harnessed if you know how to code.
- Python is the easiest programming language that you can learn. Aside from the fact that this language is used by Facebook, Google, Twitter, Instagram, and other top tech companies today, Python is an ideal language to learn for beginners because it values an open source community and sharing.
- In Python programming, functions are used to divide the code into functional groups or blocks, which will allow you to make the code more readable and more organized.
- Among the benefits of Python as a programming language is its simplicity to control containers.
- In Python, you can manipulate the strings via string operators, which are represented by familiar mathematical symbols: +, - , * , = , and /.
- In any programming language, you can use different control structures or loops, which allow for more sophisticated paths.
- Modules will allow you to systematically organize your codes by categorizing related code into a module.
- In Python, you can use basic functions and methods

needed to manipulate the files. You can execute most of the file manipulation through a file object.

In the next part of this book, we will learn more about Object-Oriented Programming and why it is crucial in your journey on learning how to code. But before that, you should try the exercises in the next chapter.

Chapter 11 - Exercises

Exercise 1 - Functions

In this first exercise, we will use a current function, and while adding your own to build a valid code:

- Add a function named list_advantages() which returns the strings:
  - "Easy to share code", "Easy to read code", "More logical code"
- Include a function named build_sentence(info) that will receive one argument that contains a string and will result to a sentence that starts with the provided string and ends with the string "is an advantage of Python!"
- Run and see how functions can work together within a single code.

Exercise 2 - Loops

Use loops to print out all odd numbers from the numbers list in the same sequence they are received. Skip any numbers, which comes after 237 in the series:

script.py

```
1 ▾  numbers = [
2          951, 402, 984, 651, 360, 69, 408, 319, 601, 485, 980,
       507, 725, 547, 544,
3          615, 83, 165, 141, 501, 263, 617, 865, 575, 219, 390,
       984, 592, 236, 105, 942, 941,
4          386, 462, 47, 418, 907, 344, 236, 375, 823, 566, 597,
       978, 328, 615, 953, 345,
5          399, 162, 758, 219, 918, 237, 412, 566, 826, 248, 866,
       950, 626, 949, 687, 217,
6          815, 67, 104, 58, 512, 24, 892, 894, 767, 553, 81, 379,
       843, 831, 445, 742, 717,
7          958, 609, 842, 451, 688, 753, 854, 685, 93, 857, 440,
       380, 126, 721, 328, 753, 470,
8          743, 527
9    ]
10
11   # your code goes here
```

Exercise 3 - Modules

Print a list in alphabetical order for the list of all functions in the module re containing the term find.

```
1    import re
2
3    # Your code goes here
```

28

PART II - INTRODUCTION TO OBJECT ORIENTED PROGRAMMING

Chapter 12 - Paradigms in Programming

There are four major paradigms in programming: logical, imperative, functional, and object-oriented.

In general, you can code anything using any paradigm, but specific types of applications are more ideal to be coded in using a certain paradigm.

Logical Paradigm

The Logical Paradigm adapts a declarative system in solving a problem. In this programming, you have to consider different logical arguments in a situation to establish facts before making queries. The computer's role in this paradigm is to maintain data and deduct logic.

There are three sections in logical programming:

1. A sequence of declarations / definitions, which define the domain of the problem
2. Statement of goals in query form
3. Statement of established facts

The program will return any deductible solution to specified queries, while the declarations and the definitions are built completely from the relations such as A is part of B or C is between A and D.

There are two main benefits of using logical programming:
1. The number of steps are minimal because the system itself can solve the problem

2. It is easy to prove the validity of a specific program

Below is an example of a code written in logical paradigm:

```
Domains
      being = symbol
Predicates
      animal(being)  %  all  animals  are
beings
      cat(being) % all cats are beings
      die(being) % all beings die
Clauses
      animal(X) :- cat(X) % all cats are
animals
      cat(dorris). % dorris is a cat
      die(X)  :-  animal(X)  %  all  animals
die
```

Imperative Paradigm

In imperative paradigm, it is assumed that a computer has the capacity to adapt to any change in the process for computation. The computer will execute calculations through a guided series of steps wherein these variables are changed or referred. It is crucial that the steps are in proper order as one wrong step will result to a different outcome depending on the existing variable values if you execute the step.

Many popular programming languages are based on an imperative paradigm, mainly because the imperative paradigm is the closest to the actual computer itself. And because of this resemblance, the imperative paradigm was the preferred choice of programmers until object-oriented paradigm was introduced.

However, the syntax for imperative programming could be difficult to prove or understand, and so debugging could be a bit difficult. And as we have mentioned earlier, proper order is essential, which does not always suit itself to most coding problems.

Functional Paradigm

In functional programming, all subprograms are viewed as functions in a mathematical perspective. They take in arguments and return one solution. The returned solution is completely based on the input, and the time at which the function called is irrelevant. Hence, the computational paradigm refers to the reduction and application.

Functional programming has been established according to functional paradigm. These languages allow functional solutions to problems by allowing a programmer to consider functions as first-class objects, so they can be considered as data, assumed to have the value of their return. Hence, they could be passed to other functions as returned from functions or arguments.

Below are the benefits of functional programming:

- It has no dependence on assignment operations, which allow programs to be assessed in various orders. This is the main reason why functional programming is often used in coding massive computers.

- It has no assignment operations, so it becomes more amenable for mathematical proof and evaluation compared to the imperative program as functional programs are more transparent.
- It gets rid of the probability of too many errors because the high-level abstraction suppresses details of programming.

On the other hand, some programmers don't prefer functional paradigm because this is considered as less efficient. Meanwhile, problems also involve different variables or sequential activities, which is ideal to handle with object-oriented or imperative programming.

Below is a sample functional code:

Function for computing the average of two numbers:

```
(defun avg(X Y) (/ (+ X Y) 2.0))
```

Function is called by:

```
> (avg 10.0 20.0)
```

Function returns:

```
15.0
```

Object-Oriented Programming (OOP)

In Object-Oriented Programming (OOP), actual objects are regarded as specific entities with their own state and exclusively modified by integrated procedures known as methods.

Because objects are independently operating, these are contained within the modules that both encapsulated the methods and local environments. The communication with an object is performed through message passing.

Objects are categorized as classes, from which they are inheriting methods and variables. Object programming is popular because it can extend and reuse codes. Python is an example of an Object-Oriented Programming.

Chapter 13 - The Four Pillars of Object-Oriented Programming

There are four pillars of Object-Oriented Programming - Abstraction, Encapsulation, Inheritance, and Polymorphism.

1. Abstraction refers to the process of exposing important feature of an object while concealing other details that are not relevant. Abstraction is crucial in programming as it can reduce the complexity of the code and it also makes the code visually pleasant.

2. Encapsulation is somehow connected to Data Hiding. This refers to the process of hiding your internal data modules as well as other implementation mechanisms from other modules. This is also a good way to limit access to specific component or properties. But be sure to take note that encapsulation is not data hiding, but data hiding is a product of encapsulation.

3. Inheritance refers to the ability of generating a new class from a current class. As the name suggests, this ability allows the code to pass on property, in which the base class or the existing class (also known as the Parent class) can transfer methods and properties, which will be inherited by the subtype or child pass. Inheritance also refers to the method of using current objects.

4. Polymorphism refers to the ability of an OOP language to take into various stages or forms. Hence, a subclass could define its own special behavior and still share the same behavior or functions of its base or parent class. It is true that a subclass could have its own behavior and also show

the same behavior from its parent class. But this is not true the other way around, because the parent class cannot copy the behavior of the child class.

Chapter 14 - Python as an OOP Language

Python is developed as an Object-Oriented Programming language, so it is easy to create and use objects and classes. It is important to have a good grasp of OOP so you can easily learn how to code using Python.

In Python, the class statement will create a new class definition. The class name immediately follows the keyword class then followed by a colon:

```
class ClassName:
    'Optional class documentation string'
    class_suite
```

The *ClassName.__doc__* can be used to to access the documentation string while the class_suite is composed of all the component statements that define class members, data functions and attributes.

In order to generate class instances, you need to call the class that uses name and pass that the *its____init___* method arguments can accept.

```
"This will generate first object of Student class"
stu1 = Student("Michael", 1995)
"This would create second object of Student class"
stu2 = Student("Sam", 1998)
```

In order to access the attributes of an object, you can use the dot operator with object. You can access the class variable via class name.

```
stu1.displayStudent()
stu2.displayStudent()
print "Total Student %d" % Student.empCount
```

In Python, each class keeps following the built-in attributes and you can access this using the dot operator similar to any other attribute –

- **__dict__**: A dictionary that contains the namespace class
- **__doc__**: Contains class documentation string
- **__module__**: defines the class. In interactive mode, this is __main__
- **__name__**: Refers to the name of the class

In Python programming, the data part refers to the variables that are linked to the namespaces of the objects and classes. These names are verified inside these objects and classes only, hence the name.

The two forms of data fields are object variables and class variables that are classified based on the ownership of the object or the class.

Every object will get a copy of the data. Hence, these are unrelated

On the other hand, class variables can be accessed via all class instances. There is only a single copy of the variable and once any of the object make modification on a variable, this will be detected by other instances.

Chapter 15 - Bringing It All Together

We now have discussed the different aspects of objects and classes and the different terminologies related with it. We also have seen the advantages and disadvantages of OOP as a programming paradigm. Python is mainly an OOP language, and to help you learn how to code, you should understand these concepts.

In summary, we have also learned the following:

- There are four programming paradigms: logical, imperative, functional, and object-oriented.
- You can learn how to code using any paradigm, but so far, object-oriented paradigm is regarded as the simplest and easiest to learn, thus recommended for beginners.
- In Object-Oriented Programming, actual objects are regarded as specific entities with their own state and exclusively modified by integrated procedures known as methods.
- The four pillars of OOP are Abstraction, Encapsulation, Inheritance, and Polymorphism.
- The two types of data fields are object variables and class variables that are classified based on the ownership of the object or the class.
- Object variables are owned by each instance or object in the class, so every object has its own copy of the data, while class variables can be accessed via all class instances.

PART III - ESSENTIAL PROGRAMMING TOOLS

Chapter 16 - Bash Script

A Bash script is basically a data file that contains a sequence of commands, which you can usually code, but will save you time if you don't. Take note that in programming, any code that you could normally run on the command line could be placed on the script, and it will be executed precisely as it is. Likewise, any code that you could be placed into a script can also normally be executed exactly as it is.

There can be many processes manifesting one program performing in memory simultaneously. For instance, you can use two terminals and still run command prompt at the same time. In such case, there will be two command prompt processes that are existing at the same time within the system. When they complete the execution, the system can terminate them so there will be no more processes that are representing the command prompt.

When you are using the terminal, you can run the Bash script to provide you a shell. When you initiate a script, it will not actually execute in this process, but rather will begin a new process to be executed inside. But as a beginner in programming, you don't really need to worry too much about the mechanism of this script as running Bash can be very easy.

You may also encounter in some tutorials about script execution, which is pretty much the same thing. Before executing the script, it should have permission in place, as the program will return an error message if you fail to grant permission.

Below is a sample Bash script:

```
#!/bin/bash
# declare STRING variable
STRING="Hello Python"
#print variable on a screen
echo $STRING
```

You can use the 755 shorthand so you can modify the script and make sure that you can share it to others to execute the script.

Chapter 17 - Python RegEx

RegEx refers to the regular expression that defines the string of text, which allows you to generate patterns in managing, matching, and locating text. Python is a good example of a programming language, which uses regex. Regex can also be utilized in text editors and from the command line to search for a text inside a file.

When you first encounter regex, you might think that it is a different programming language. But mastering regex could save you tons of hours if you are working with the text or you require parse large amounts of data.

The re module provides complete support for regex in Python. It also increases the exception re.error if there is an error while using or compiling a regex. There are two essential functions that you have to know in using regex for Python. But before that, you should understand that there are different characters that have special meaning when they are used in regular expression. So you will not be confused in working with regex, we will use r'expression' when we mean Raw Strings.

The two important functions in Python regex are the search and match functions.

The search function looks for the first instance of an RE pattern inside a string with optional flags. Below is the syntax for the search function:

```
re.search(pattern, string, flags=0)
```

43

The search function has the following parameters:

String - will be searched in order to match the pattern within the string

Pattern - regex to be matched

Flags - modifiers that can be specified using bitwise

The re.search function can return an object match if successful, and object none if failed. You should use groups() or groups(num) function of object match to find a matched expression.

Below is an example of a code using the search function:

```python
#!/usr/bin/python
import re

line = "Cats are smarter than dogs";

matchObj = re.match( r'dogs', line, re.M|re.I)
if matchObj:
   print "match --> matchObj.group() : ", matchObj.group()
else:
   print "No match!!"

searchObj = re.search( r'dogs', line, re.M|re.I)
if searchObj:
   print "search --> searchObj.group() : ", searchObj.group()
else:
   print "Nothing found!!"
```

Meanwhile, the match function will try to match the RE pattern in order to string with specific flags. Below is the syntax for the match function:

```python
re.match(pattern, string, flags=0)
```

The match function has the following parameters:

String - this will be searched to match the pattern at the

start of the string

       Pattern - this is the regex to be matched

       Flags - modifiers that can be specified using bitwise

Below is an example code using a match function:

```python
#!/usr/bin/python
import re

line = "Cats are smarter than dogs"

matchObj = re.match( r'(.*) are (.*?) .*', line, re.M|re.I)

if matchObj:
    print "matchObj.group() : ", matchObj.group()
    print "matchObj.group(1) : ", matchObj.group(1)
    print "matchObj.group(2) : ", matchObj.group(2)
else:
    print "No match!!"
```

Chapter 18 - Python Package Manager

In programming, package managers refer to the tools used to automate the system of installing, configuring, upgrading, and uninstalling programs for a specific language's system in an orderly manner.

Also known as a package management system, it also deals with the distribution and archiving of data files including the name of the software, version, number, purpose and a sequence of dependencies needed for the language to properly run.

When you use a package manager, the metadata will be archived in the local database usually to avoid code mismatches and missing permissions.

In Python, you can use a utility to locate, install, upgrade and eliminate Python packages. It can also identify the most recent version of a package installed on the system as well as automatically upgrade the current package from a remote or local server.

Python Package Manager is not free and you can only use it through ActivePython. It also utilizes repositories, which are group of pre-installed packages and contain different types of modules.

Chapter 19 - Source Control

In programming, a source control (also known as version control or revision control), manages the changes to the codes, which is identified by a letter or number code regarded as the revision number or just revision. For instance, an initial set of code is known as revision 1, and then the first modification will be revision 2. Every revision will be linked with a timestamp as well as the person who made the change. Revisions are important so the code could be restored or compared.

Source control is important if you are working with a team. You can combine your code changes with other code changes done by a developer through different views that will show detailed changes, then combine the proper code into the primary code branch.

Source control is crucial for coding projects regardless if you are using Python or other languages. Take note that each coding project should start by using a source control system such as Mercurial or Git.

Various source control systems have been developed ever since the existence of programming. Before, proprietary control systems provided features that are customized for large coding projects and particular project workflows. But today, open sourcer systems can be used for source control regardless if you are working on a personal code or as part of a large team.

It is ideal to use an open source version control system in your early Python codes. You can use either Mercurial or Git, which are both open source and used for distributing source control.

Subversion is also available, which can be used to centralize the system to check files and minimize conflicting merges.

Chapter 20 - Bringing It All Together

Programming tools will make your work easier. The tools discussed in this part will save you a lot of time, collaborate easier, and make your codes seamless. In summary, we have learned the following:

- A Bash Script can save you a lot of coding time and will make your code lines more organized and readable.
- Regular Expressions or RegEx can help you find, search, and match strings of text inside your codes so you don't have to browse line by line or analyze each code on your own.
- Package Managers will automate the system to easily install, upgrade, configure or remove specific programs that could aid your coding work
- Source Control is crucial to manage the revisions, regardless if you are working alone or with a team so you can restore changes or compare revisions.

You can still work on your codes without these tools but your life will be easier if you choose to use them.

PART IV - INTRODUCTION TO COMPUTER SCIENCE

Chapter 21 - Data Structures

Data Structure refers to the arrangement of data in the memory of a computer or storage of a disk. Common types of data structures are hash tables, binary trees, stacks, queues, linked lists, and arrays.

Hash Table

A hash table refers to the data structure that keeps data associatively. In this structure, the data is archived in array manner in which every data value has its own special index value. Knowing the index of a specified data will makes it easy for data access.

Tree

As a data structure, a tree signifies the nodes linked by edges. A common format of this structure is the binary tree, which is a special data structure used specifically for data storage. However, every node should have a max of two children. Using binary tree has the advantages of both a linked list and an ordered array as finding data is as fast as in a sorted array and deletion or insertion are easy as in linked list.

Stack

This data structure is named as a stack, because it behaves similar to a real-world stack such as a pile of plates or a deck of cards. However, a real-world stack will only allow operations on one end. For instance, we could place or discard a plate or card only from the stock. Similarly, a stack data structure will only allow data operations on one end. Hence, you can only access the data contained on the top of the stack.

Queue

A queue data structure somehow behaves like a stack, but unlike in stacks, a queue is open at both ends. One end is used for inserting data while the other is used for discarding data. This data structure follows the FIFO principle or First In First Out, that is the data item stored first will be accessed first.

Linked List

A linked list refers to a series of data structures that are linked together through links. Every link keeps a connection to another link. This data structure is a popular form, next to array.

Array

Array refers to the container that could keep a fix number of data and these data must be of the same type. Many of the data structures are using arrays to execute their algorithms, which we will learn in the next chapter.

Chapter 22 - Algorithms

Algorithm refers to the sequenced process that defines instructions to be performed in a specific order to obtain the desired result. In general, algorithms are generated as separate elements from the programming language used. Hence, an algorithm can be performed using any language.

Take note that there is no established standard in creating algorithms. Instead, it is dependent on the resource and the problem. Also remember that algorithms are not generated to provide support for any specific programming code. Most languages follow similar constructs such as control flow (if--else) or loops (for, do, while).

Writing algorithm takes a process and should be executed after defining the problem domain. Therefore, you should first understand the problem field that you are trying to design a solution.

You can learn more about writing an algorithm through an example. Let us say that we have to create an algorithm that will enable the code to add two numbers then print the result.

```
Step 1 - Begin
step 2 - identify three integers x, y & z
step 3 - define values of x & y
step 4 - add values of x & y
step 5 - keep output of step 4 to z
step 6 - print z
step 7 - STOP
```

This algorithm will be able to tell you how you can code your program. You can also write this algorithm as:

```
Step 1 - BEGIN ADD
step 2 - get values of x & y
step 3 - z ← x + y
step 4 - show c
step 5 - STOP
```

PART V - CODING AS A CAREER

Chapter 23 - Best Practices in Programming

Similar to any industry, there are best practices in programming that you can follow so you can create cleaner, more professional, and useful codes.

First Things First: Structure Your Repository

Most programmers, regardless of the language they are using will start a new program by structuring first their repositories on top of the source control. You can choose to use any source control you deem suitable for your program, but when it comes to your repository, you have to focus on the project.

For example in Python, there are several important components that must be set up, and you must devote some time in generating each of these, at least in skeletal structure, before you even enter your first line of code.

The usual repository structure in Python will look like this:

```
docs/conf.py
docs/index.rst
module/__init__.py
module/core.py
tests/core.py
LICENSE
README.rst
Requirements.txt
setup.py
```

Be Consistent in Creating Documentation

Although you may think that it can be too much work, consistency in your documentation is key in writing a clean code. Fortunately, the community of Python programmers has made this process quite easy, and it includes the use of three basic concepts and tools: Sphinx, Docstrings, and reStructuredText.

Always Fix Broken Windows

The Broken Windows Theory is a theory in criminology, which states that the proper monitoring and maintenance of a city requires creating a more positive environment to prevent crimes. Even though this theory is still being debated on, it receives some merit in the world of programming.

In particular, when you are creating your codes, it is ideal to always fix the broken codes or broken windows immediately when you see them. Ignoring the error and moving on to a new module or component could and will usually lead to more complicated errors.

Master PyPI

Although you can produce clean and functional codes using documentation methods and proper syntax, it is ideal to use Python Package Index or PyPI, which is a tool for module repository.

Most projects will initially start by using current projects on PyPI, and with hundreds of times of writing to select from, there is always the possibility that you will find the code that is suitable for your project.

Chapter 24 - How to Find a Job as a Coder

As I have mentioned in the beginning of this ebook, programmers are highly in demand in the current job market. Few people know how to program, but landing a job as a programmer without any experience can be a real challenge.

Here are some tips that can help you better prepare yourself to find that first programmer job.

Work On Your Portfolio

Once you have already learned the basics of coding, you should start building things, which will show your coding skills. Be sure to include important coding projects on your CV so your potential employers will have a better idea on what you can do.

Publish a Blog

It might be impossible to become the best programmer in the world, but still you can market yourself by publishing a blog. You can choose to write about your experiences on learning how to code. Writing about the things that you are learning is a good opportunity to show that you are interested in learning new things. This will also provide your recruiters something to discuss over. In addition, blogging about what you have learned will somehow crystallize your learnings.

Open a GitHub Account

As a programmer, it is ideal if you have a GitHub account. If you don't have a Computer Science degree or if you don't have any related experience, you may find it difficult to prove that you could do the job. You can showcase your coding skills through GitHub.

Your Web Presence

Make sure that your online profiles in Facebook, Twitter, and LinkedIn will show that you are a programmer. Recruiters are now checking on the social profiles of the potential employees so make sure that your accounts will represent your professionalism.

Attend Events

As much as possible try to attend relevant events such as conferences, hackatons, and local programmer meetups. Through these events, you can start networking to people who are connected to people who can provide you a job. You will also get a good grasp of what the local scene is for programmers. Many recruiters are also attending coding events when they are looking for new talents.

Chapter 25 - Becoming Part of a Team

There's a big chance that when you find a job as a programmer, you will work in a team where you need to perform a certain role and do your part to achieve goals. Yes, you may have to do your codes alone, but you should still learn what makes a good team and the essence of teamwork in programming.

When you are already getting a good grasp of coding, it becomes exciting so it may be enticing to concentrate your own goals, or even the audacity to show to your team mates that you are better then then. In fact, even in programming, some developers think that they will stand out if they compete with each other. To some extent that can help for the growth of the team, but if the competition is too much, the purpose of teamwork may be lost.

Even though individual skills is crucial, most programming managers will prioritize team performance. Remember, being the best player for the lowest-ranked basketball team makes no sense. Of course, everyone will know that you are the best programmer in your team, but still your team is a loser.

You can only do as much as an individual programmer. Even the best programmer in the world needs a team because a person only has a maximum threshold for effectiveness. A valuable programmer is the one who makes everyone else in the team feel that they are valued.

If you really want to stand out and still be the type of programmer that is welcome to have in their team, be the kind of programmer who care about the performance of the group rather than his own personal credits.

This involves classic attitude towards teamwork such as honesty, constructive communication, synergy, and group mindset.

Chapter 26 - Further Learning

Learning the basic of programming is just the beginning of your journey in the exciting digital world. You have barely scratched the surface.

After learning to code using Python, it is time to take a higher notch by taking advanced courses in programming. Python alone offers a lot of higher levels that you will take years to master.

You should also try learning how to code using other programming languages such as Java, JavaScript, C, C#, C++, and more.

The key to master any skill is to never stop learning. This is quite easy to achieve in programming as every day, you have the chance to solve problems and work out using your own solutions.

After some years of doing codes, you will eventually improve your skills, which you can use to land a better job. Your problem solving skills will also greatly improve, which you can use as a key selling point if you are looking for a job in other fields.

Also, you may try to take formal programming courses. There are community colleges and night school that are offering these courses regardless of your age, background, or income.

Alternatively, you can also try online courses that are offered for free. The best programming courses are offered by CodeAcademy, Coursera, and Udemy.

Chapter 27 - Next Steps

Now that you have finished the basic lessons in programming, what will be your next step?

There are a lot of opportunities and things that you can do if you know how to code:

- You can become an entry-level programmer in a company where you can work with a team for exciting projects.
- You can become an entrepreneur by developing programs that can offer solutions to every day problems of regular people, businesses, or even other programmers.
- You can develop your own mobile apps, website, software and other electronic products built from codes that you can sell in the market
- You can teach young kids how to code
- You can take a shot and apply as a programmer in big tech companies such as Google, Facebook, Twitter, etc.

The possibilities are endless. As Steve Jobs once said, "you can't connect the dots looking forward; you can only connect them looking backwards. So you have to trust that the dots will somehow connect in your future."

The key is to be persistent and never stop learning how to code.

www.ingramcontent.com/pod-product-compliance
Lightning Source LLC
Chambersburg PA
CBHW070857070326
40690CB00009B/1881